SMALL BIRD

poems and prayers

SMALL BIRD

poems and prayers

Elizabeth Cunningham

STATION HILL / BARRYTOWN, LTD.

Published by Station Hill / Barrytown, Ltd. in Barrytown, NY 12507.

E-mail: publishers@stationhill.org
Online catalogue: http://www.stationhill.org

Station Hill Arts is a project of The Institute for Publishing Arts, Inc., a not-for-profit, federally tax exempt organization in Barrytown, New York, which gratefully acknowledges ongoing support for its publishing program from the New York State Council on the Arts.

Designed by Susan Quasha

Library of Congress Cataloging-in-Publication Data

Cunningham, Elizabeth, 1953-
   Small bird : poems and prayers / Elizabeth Cunningham.
      p. cm.
   ISBN 1-58177-058-8 (acid-free paper)
      I. Title.

PS3553.U473 S62 2000
811'.54—dc21   99-054908

CONTENTS

In loving memory of my mother
EMILY ELIZABETH MEEKER CUNNINGHAM
September 4, 1922 - March 27, 1997

ACKNOWLEDGMENTS

Thanks from my heart to my friend Cait Johnson, poet and midwife of poetry, mistress of titles, whose keen vision and intuition helped shape this book.

Thank you also to the Women's Wisdom Council where many of these poems were first offered and received.

Heart Prayer

You can only pray what's in your heart

so if your heart is being ripped from your chest
pray the tearing

if your heart is full of bitterness
pray it to the last dreg

if your heart is a river gone wild
pray the torrent

or a lava flow scorching the mountain
pray the fire

pray the scream in your heart
the fanning bellows

pray the rage, the murder
and the mourning

pray your heart into the great quiet hands that can hold it
like the small bird it is.

1

WILL TO SING

Bird Feeder

I want to write a poem
it hurts that bad
but I have no images
except old old ones like
my heart is broken
really it feels more like it's been ripped
out of my chest
when I look I see gold
talons and a bloody mess.

What will you do with my heart
old bird? Have it
right there on the grass
or is this to go
home to some crag
I can never climb?

When I look I see it
slide soft down a
baby bird's gorge
and that's fine.

Take it, it's yours, old
bird with your black
all-seeing eye
you cruise the air currents
like god and I think
how free
and all the time you're just like me
hungry.

Here

When I am here
in this heavy-lidded place,
beneath my eyes the fluid
trapped so I can hardly see
and my body is packed, wet sand
and I hear nothing but the silent
pull of the whirlpool,
I can just remember
that mountain place where
the bird sounds are bright
as morning and the cows wear bells
and on the shore the waves
bring such relief erasing
all that went before. I remember
that place. I remember
when I am there my body
is an empty bowl singing with power.
All I need is one note to get there.
But when I am here
I have no will to sing.

Will

Sometimes surrender means
not letting go when you want
to let the current take you let
the waves close over you let
death come with its sweet
blackness like night
in your mother's womb like
a whole bottle of dark wine.
Sometimes surrender means
walking into the wind
clawing your way up a cliff
or running in place your whole
life while the world tumbles by
and nothing you do
seems to make any difference.
Sometimes surrender means
not to give up but to give
one more ounce of strength
one more pound of flesh
your crazy stubborn will.

Defendant

When the D.A. sums it all up
I can feel the weight of my own heart sinking
and the prison hunched shoulders begin to make
and I feel sick knowing
I'd have to say guilty
though I did not want him to be,

the tall black man whose back
I watched for two weeks, who turned
to smile at me twice, three times,
who wore an ankh on his chest
like mine, who had no reason
to tell anyone the truth
who blew it one more time.
I didn't want him to be

guilty. I wanted him to be
a suffering innocent
exonerated at last.
There were no innocents
are no innocents or else
we all are just by being born
by not knowing what the hell
is going on why
we're here at all.

Fall

We plop like fat acorns
or waft for miles on the wind
like milkweed seeds before
we light, but we fall, we fall
like the comet with its life-coded tail
like angels with an attitude
like our fathers into our mothers
murky depths we fall
to this place this planet this
rock soil sea seedbed
where gods elbow each other
for a ringside seat to see us
break open and grow.

Torch Singer

Forget what you see
the real me is wearing
a skimpy, sequined dress
overflowed by my breasts.
My finger and toe nails glitter
I'm in a dive full of low light and life
and blue smoke
and I'm singing.
My voice is dark
with something shining in it
like the scotch I'm drinking.

And when I sing
your sorrows flow into my song
like tributaries and I pay tribute
to them all.
When I sing my throat is huge
and blue as the sky.
I can hold the whole world
in one note
then let it fly.

2

IN MY SMALLNESS

Prayer

O great mystery
take me to the deep place
where the root drinks dark water.
Take me to the ocean floor
where the currents sway sea forests.
Show me the high places, too,
where the eagle rests on wind
and clouds tumble slowly
in their hugeness.
O mother father mystery
I am a fretful child
flailing in my smallness.
Take me to your breast.
Let me ride the swells
of your slow, deep
breath.

Message

When I come with my questions
to his feet
— his feet that are the color of new-turned earth
in slanting light, his feet
that touch the earth and know its soul
in their soles — he sits me down
and turns me around so I lean
against his knees, then
he points past me.
Even around his finger I can see
those winds that swirl the blue earth
I am afraid to look, but I do.

I see my little self. There is
an awful lot of sighing going on
and downcast looks as I sit
— for most of my life —
wondering if I can write
if I'm doing it right.

Beyond me I hear huge surf.
There is a big wind and a small seed.
There are purple winter briars
and lively spring weeds.
There is sky after sky.

Words? I ask. Translation?
I want to show you the huge things,
he says, and the small things.
When you are small
the world is huge
when you are big
the world shrinks to nothing.
Be a tiny seed tossed on the wind
take yourself lightly.

W(h)ine

Over and over I prayed my complaint
(Job has nothing on me)
How many times can I be crushed
dear god before permanent damage is done and I never get up again
I'm afraid my god (so afraid)
that one more time will do it
been too many times too many
years, god, ya know I'm not
as young as I used to be.
And I went to sleep with
the whine of my prayer in my ears.

I woke too early (geez, can't I
even get some decent sleep?) and
in the wide-eyed dawn the answer came:

*The grapes must be crushed
to be made into wine.*

Then I saw the beautiful, stained feet of god
        dancing   dancing
in all my despairs, and I glimpsed
the rich, dark wine to come and
tasted it on god's tongue.

Divine Love

Dear one, dreadful one
maybe this emptiness is only
the hugeness of your love.
In my plunging terror
I am too small to touch it.
Beloved, please, gather it up
in a hazelnut so I can hold it
tightly in my hand.

Siren

I am needed, I am needed
is the ego's siren song.

So when it wails
let your lungs fill with sky,
your hands open like rivers
into the sea.
Let your heart burn fiercely
and the ash of your old, shed skins
will feed the earth.

Prayer for a Sound Ego

O love,
bless the ego that gives us
form and strength.
May it be humble and merry,
always bending to the breath
of your spirit,
always delighting in the grace
of your dance.

Dinosaurs

The dinosaurs are not gone.
It comforts me to know that
when I crave my own extinction.

As a child, I feared them.
I did not want to see
their big, old bones in that stuffed
stuffy museum, because I knew
they were just waiting to find
their huge, green flesh again
and then find me.

I'd be hidden in a drawer
under the rectory window seat
while they hunted,
their thudding feet bigger
than the driveway,
their ugly heads higher
than the church steeple.

But now they comfort me
even the condor, biggest of all,
is light with hollow bones
and all but the buzzard,
champion rider of the wind,
has its own cry or song.
I collect their feathers,
grown first for warmth,
then adapted for flight
in the most brilliant
evolutionary move
till the whales said fuck it
and returned to the sea.

Dear singing, soaring dinosaurs
take me under your wing, teach me,
the heavy-boned and sorrow-bound,
how to lighten
up.

Wind

Sometimes the way I know
god loves me is the wind.
I'll be sitting outside
praying why how what
and a big wind will come up
come right up in my face
lift the hairs on my scalp
count them maybe
or maybe not maybe
it's just loving like when
someone tousles your hair
or a dog licks your face.
And I say, oh, you *are* there
and god says yes
didn't you know?

Journey: Spring Equinox

When I come through the soft red folds
to the other world, I am still inside
some glowing place of membrane
but the light is so strong
I find my strength, the hardness
of beak and bone and I begin
to peck and beat my way home
to sky.

Later I take flying lessons.
My teacher tells me,
First you fall and then you find
your wings. Wings are balance
born in your shoulder blades.
When you need to rest
ride the wind. The wind
is your mother, the wind
is a breast.

Sky

I love the sky
nothing else is big enough.

I love how I forget it sometimes
take it for granted
like it was some big old ceiling
then it swoops down in a
grey swirl leaves spiraling
birds crossing to safety
winged boats to harbor.

I love how it draws me up
when I look
how sky blue can be brittle or soft
how it blooms in morning glories
in the last days before the first frost.

I love how the stars
dim and sharpen
how the moon rolls around
and around
losing and finding itself
in different quarters
different lights.

Somebody please
let me be a leaf
flying so high in the sky
I can't see myself
anymore.

3

RIVER RUNNING THROUGH ME

The River Stick

I sit in a nest of tidal roots
under leaves lit by light on water,
their dapple changing
with ripple and wind.
A long, curving stick rests lightly
in the same crux that cradles me.
Here take it, says the river.
Oh, no thank you (I am polite)
it looks so lovely where it is.
It's not as if it will stay here,
reasons the river, take it
to remember me by
the way I meander
the grain of my flow
the peace you know
when you're with me.

Translation

God speaks Arabic,
Muslims say, everything else
is translation.
Arabic is beautiful
like the sound of a stream
of a particular size,
not too many rocks
just the right number
to make the syllables distinct,
not too wide so the water
has strength and thrust
as it flows between grassy banks,
through beds of reeds.

This is my translation
of the Koran

and also I hear the low, bird sounds
from the birds who hold
the stream's song
in their throats.

The Table of the Gods

Some days I find myself
on the table of the gods.
They come when I am
laid bare,
a sacrifice, a feast.
Be still, someone says.
Then I sense what I call
their hands,
though it's more like
gravity,
a river running through me
slow, heavy, sweet,
pouring from my feet.
And I breathe O love
O love
until they are done.

Psalm

Meet me half way
holy one
for I have been walking a long time
in dry places
where the earth cracks and opens
onto nothing.
I have seen the shine of poison leaves
in dull noon glare
and I have been alone
not believing anymore
in you.

Today I have been singing your names
your many names.
I have arced my spine
like a green stem
like a young tree.
I have said: cool water, flow here
healing water, come.
I have hollowed myself for you
I have made an empty place
for gladness, for shouts
of joy.

Come now, holy one.
I am here in the valley
under your mountain.
I am not afraid of death
or its shadow.
I only want to hear the bells of your goats
ringing   ringing:
The holy one is coming
she who dwells in secret

whose face is more than moon
more than sun.
The holy one is coming
is welling within me
is here.

Peace

The problem is
people think peace is boring
we have lost our imagi-
nations. We have forgotten
the fluidity of peace
how it is like all the muscles
rippling to lift the dancer's leg,
how it is the slow rhythm of tidal rivers
how it is clouds forming and dispersing
how it is a flock of birds turning as one
in evening sky
how it is food laid out on a round table
and honest struggle
between lovers and friends
how it pulses in our blood
how it sings in our ears
how the death of each tiny thing
is held secure in its arms
with the life. We have forgotten
how boring it is to kill each other
how predictable.
There is much more suspense
in peace.

What if

What if my heart is an opening rose
      and god is a honeybee gathering sweetness.

What if my mind is the crown of a tree
      and god is a wind raging there.

What if my soul is a deep root
      and god is my dark food and drink.

Did We?

I lie down to offer my prayers for healing,
not feeling so hot myself
the faces of everyone I know
drift by my third eye
as my hands grow hot
on all the places that hurt
coming to rest at my heart
where they are met with fire
not their own.

Then the fire floods me
entering every opening
till all I am is opening
for this hard sweet heat
that fills me.
Is it you? I ask
Are you doing what I think
you're doing? Yes.
What do I do? Just open
open nothing less.

I do and I come in a trembling
column from crux to heart.
Did we just do what I think we did?
Yes. Feeling better now?
Yes Yes.

Echoing

I walk the beach in early morning
moon dissolving, tide low.
I walk between worlds
of earth and water
where the sea pulls back her skirt
just a little
to show some of her secrets.
Everything echoes and reflects.
I breathe my own female scent
in mud flats; sky shines
in tidal pools. Ripples
in the sand echo the shape of waves
the shape of light darting over them
the shape of gull wings and wing shadow.
Tiny tidal rivulets snake to the sea
patterned like snake bones.
I feel the pull of low tide and waning moon
low in my womb where the blood
should have flowed a week ago
but didn't. In my new arrhythm
I hear the the sea's wild syncopation
at the turning of the tide.
I search the sea's floor for secrets
echoed in my ebbing flow.

Dyeing

When I dyed my hair red
the goo was like blood
not the thin kind that comes
from a cut but clotted, viscous
like blood from the womb
blood that's flowed through
soft, damp caverns, the kind
of blood gods muck with.

I'd scoop it up with my fingers
and smear it all over my hair
it felt like fingerpainting
and my head turned slick and dark
as a newborn ploughing the red walls
the red waves.

I'm letting it go now, blood color
seeping slowly into my old earth
brown with its bare hint of red
a trace element in the soil.
I will miss my dyeing rite
the blood in the bowl
on my hands
on my skull.

4

TRANSIENT SKY

Flower Light

At twilight I watch the black-eyed susans.
The grass and trees have gone grey,
the sky and the river, grey,
but the susans still hold their color.
I want to catch the moment
it disappears, so I do not
look at the lemon-wedge moon
or the first faint stars. I find
the yellow does not drift away
like a stick on the river
or scent on the air.
It dims slowly, seeping back
deep in the flower.

Then comes a moment
when the color brightens.
Maybe the moment when moonlight
overwhelms the afterglow,
the last moment of day,
the first moment of night.
The black-eyed susans shine from inside
each petals shines,
and then their light goes out.

The Old One Speaks

You must be unmade here
inside my grey cloak
inside my cold womb
here where the ice forms
and breaks
at the river's edge.

Mother's Day, 1997

Praise to my mother, who is now
        the dirt I crumble between my hands
        as I dig to plant flowers on her grave.

Praise to my mother, who is
        the moisture in that soil, who is
        the heat it holds.

Praise to my mother whose
        darkness yields the iridescent green
        that makes the sky blue.

Praise to my dead mother, who is
        young again in the giving
        of spring.

Crossroads: The Drawing

I try to draw what I saw,
the woman at the crossroads
(which is to say, me) standing alone.
But the lines do not convey my
desolation as the roads twist away
and away. Maybe you thought they were rivers.
Rivers, roads, what does it matter. They're
only metaphors for going, letting go, losing,
getting lost. And I stand still in the green
shade of my own maturity as my daughter springs
down one road and my mother flies — or swims —
up another (when you're dead you don't
have to walk). Maybe you're wondering
why the sky is red, if it is the sky.
It could be earth just as easily
or blood — Chinese Red is my most
menstrual marker. But it ran out
and Black Grape has to do for death.
There are no moons in this drawing.
My mother, my daughter, and I,
we are enough.

The Egyptian Music Video of the Dead

On my mother's birthday
(her second since she's been dead)
we plant gold chrysanthemums on her grave.
An old Madonna tape, my daughter's choice,
blares as we drive away.
When we arrive at my father's condo,
Madonna's greatest hit begins its gravitational
pull to the dance floor. Let's wait till it's done,
my daughter begs. I agree, mesmerized,
watching the best MTV I've ever seen
unroll somewhere between the windshield and my mind.

There's my mother, younger than I ever knew her,
with hair, '40s style, curled shoulder length.
Her hands meet over her head, which she moves
serpentine, side to side, matching the movement
of her hips. The whole dark shining dance floor is hers,
wide as her smile. Marina! I can't keep it to myself,
Marina! Grandma's vogueing! Whatever, Mom,
my daughter rolls her eyes, the video rolls on.
More detail comes. She's wearing some Egyptian outfit,
I report, admiring that earth-toned blue,
the way the skirt follows the shape of her hips
then flares into tiny pleats at the back around her feet.
Mom, says Marina, the men in white coats are your friends.

I keep quiet after that, my eyes wet as I watch my mother
glamorous, joyous, a forties film star, a powerful priestess.
I knew it, I knew it! What she would not let me see in life
she gives me now, on the second birthday of her death.
Someday when I'm dead, I say to my daughter
(but not out loud) I'll dance for you.
Maybe even before.

The Three Again

I walk the labyrinth
in the sunken meadow.

I hear my daughter
splashing in the pond above.

Where is my mother now?
The wind answers.

Moving Water

My mother once told me
I love the sound of moving water.
We were driving in a car
I don't know what came over her
or me. Except I had never heard her say
I love — anything but us.
Suddenly my mother was
this secret other person with a soul,
a great I-am when
I was always so afraid she wasn't.

Now my mother is nine months dead
and I am being born again
by a river. Here where the stream
spreads out in rays on runneled sand
and the river waves rush to meet it.
Now the rains stops and the mist
moves into light.

I want to look and yet
I close my eyes and let
the light rest on my lids.
I am hearing the stream
I am hearing the river
I am hearing the sea
I am hearing my mother say
I love the sound of moving water.

Noticing

When I drive my daughter to school
I notice that I am noticing
the way the wet tire marks reflect the sky
the movement of clouds
the subtle colors of November.
I notice I am noticing
without anything in the way
no obsessive thoughts
no fantasies, no lists
of all I have to do. This state
so simple and transparent
has eluded me all my life.
Descriptions of it by Buddhists
and the like enraged me.
It seemed so impossible to grasp.
It is impossible
to grasp.

Not Wasted

There are things I remember
like watching the stars come out
with my children when they were young.
How quiet and still we were.
The bats came out, too,
black and beautiful against
that transient sky — you couldn't
call it purple or blue — doing
their sonar dance with the bugs
while the birds gave a last twitter
or two. Sometimes the coracle moon
would be setting, the last light
lapping it silently.
We would watch together,
my children's mouths small
gaping nights and their eyes
that same dusk color
with the first stars floating in them.
And when I remember I know
I have not wasted my life.

Dream Poem

The poem is so beautiful.
I see the ink on the page
three rough stanzas, words
and lines slashed here and there.
At the same time I see
the world the words call into being
the world that called the words.
There are golden spires
and the poet's eye floats over them
like light, like soft pierced
clouds but

this poem is not about the spires.
Somewhere a woman is giving birth
a song is being sung
and I am trying to tell someone
look, look at the spires, listen
to this poem I am writing
I search my notebooks but
the stanzas have
separated themselves
like continents, like clouds
like mothers and children grown

beyond them.
It is the third stanza
that matters most
the last line written and re-
written where the mother greets
the new-born daughter
with lovely words like
little girl and turn, turn
like the light, like the earth
like the wind under wings
when the bird reverses
its flight.

Moon Bath

Bathing by moonlight
I see my breasts and belly
so round and bright
they could rise full and shining
in some other world's night,
a heavenly body, all right
that's me, me and the moon
and the sun all linked
by reflecting light.

Women's bodies are made
for moonlight and I know
by this light I am not alone.
My body came out of a woman's
body as another woman's body
has come out of mine woman
within woman within woman
like those Russian nesting dolls
but alive life linking life
and I wonder

did the others ever bathe
by moonlight and see the glow
of their bodies reflected
in mine?

5

RAIMENT OF THE SOUL

Hopefree

Hope is a hair shirt
that keeps you itching
and mortified.
You wear it hidden
next to the skin
and it chafes you raw,
this secret sin
of wanting.

I'm going to rip
the damn thing off
and burn it, give
hope the death
it deserves.

And don't call me hopeless.
I'm not talking about less hope
I mean no hope
none at all.

That thing with feathers?
That's not hope, that's me
hopefree-as-a-bird
you know like carefree
only better.

Robe

She takes me to the sales rack
of white terry cloth robes
upstairs in a sunny back corner
of her shop.

I do not wear bathrobes!
Not white terry cloth robes,
not my style, not
my style at all.

There is a robe here for you, she says,
one especially for you.

She rifles through the robes until
she finds the one with
large black letters sprawled inside
as if some kid had done the job
with spray-paint in the dark.

Trust
Joy

The words are still wet! They will
rub off on my back, they will
seep into my skin.

Yes, she says.
She turns away and leaves me
to choose my robe.

Minks

On a winter morning
Marina goes out to feed her rabbit
wearing my grandmother's mink coat and stole
over my mother's blue-quilted bathrobe.
Coming back down the drive
she glides on the ice as much as she can.
The dog jumps at her, excited by the antique furs
the stole made of whole animals
complete with heads and tails.
Marina defends the minks
and shoos the dog away.

Inside, she comes to show me her outfit.
We sit and talk about the coat
how old it is. I remember playing
with the stole when I was a child,
how each mink's mouth was a clasp
biting the next one's leg or tail.
We need to say a prayer for the minks
Marina says. Without embarrassment
this untaught almost teenaged child
places her hands together at her heart.

Forgive our ancestors for killing you
for taking your lives
for the sake of a coat. Forgive us
for wearing your fur
as we honor our ancestors.
We will protect your children
and your grandchildren.
When we wear this coat
we will give thanks to you for warmth.

I look in awe at this youngest
of my mother's line in her ancestral robes
how her prayer rose so surely
from her nature to embrace
foremothers and minks at once.

Raiment

FOR BETTY SANG, IN MEMORIAM

When I did not know she had already died,
I said to him — her lord and mine — Take
my love to her does she know
I love her? He said,
Your love is always with her.
Love is the raiment of the soul.
She is very well dressed and
your love is one of the garments
that becomes her best.

In my heart's eye
I see your soul resplendent.
Your face shines lovely as the new moon
above the fierce finery of sunset.
So much love   So much love
I like to think the purple shawl
threaded with gold, warmed
with a touch of red
is mine.

Fashion Statement

I sit on the bank above the stream
my prayers poured out
listening listening.
The stream flows through my ears
from left to right
the stream flows through my heart.
I close my eyes so I can hear
whatever speaks. I see
a woman squatting on the other side.
She is washing a garment
stained with blood.
The cold stream flows through the fabric
dissolving the dried particles
releasing them from the fibers
and the bright-dark stream
bears the blood away.

Across the stream from her he watches.
What am I seeing? I ask him.
When the wounds are healed,
wash the garment. Why
wear old dried blood?
See? It's gone. She holds the garment up.
But it's too cold and wet to put on, I say.
Then birds come and fly it up
to the sun and the wind.
They bring it back dry and warm.
The woman puts the garment on
and steps across the stream
to him.

Deserted

If you want me to walk this way,
you'll have to help me,
but that is supposing you are there at all
and have a will to command.
And if you have, who am I
to argue and bargain?
Isn't it more dignified to say yes
or even no?

You know, it could be that I am only
crazy or, worse, grandiose to think
that I am on speaking/listening terms
with whoever you are. Who are you anyway?
My craziness dressed up as god?
And if you are more than that,
what's your game? Did you call me?
Is there a path? Or just
the stretching desert I say I love.

Yes, this is the desert way.
And it is so beautiful.
I was going to say something about stark
reality bone truth, but
it's the illusions of desert I love,
the way the mountains seem to float in certain lights,
the way the land looks like sea.
I am seduced by loveliness and mirage,
by the way cloud shadow deepens the plain.
I am seduced by solitude and sage-smelling silence,
by the way my mind slips my skull and soars.

I've followed you — or my delusions
to this place of secret water and rattlesnake wind.
There is no shelter here from extremes

of noon or night or my own nature.
I am naked as a newborn, exposed to the elements,
and I could die as easily,
if you desert me.

6

IN YOUR TEMPLE

The House of Morning

In the house of morning
I watch the trees
the secret passageways
of light burrowing in leaves.
The wind turns the trees to ocean.
I close my eyes and everything
is white and roaring.

In the house of morning
I wait for messengers.
I sing for them
the winged ones
who turn the walls to sky
who surf the huge
breaking waves of air.

Small one, they say,
you have come to our house,
are you not afraid?
Yes, I sing, yes yes.
Then you are welcome,
they sing back, welcome
in the house of morning.

Good Friday

I went to your house today
or was it your father's house
or my father's. The place
I first met you, or
did I meet you much longer ago
before what I call me had memory?

Then you were green corn
you were golden pollen
you were the bee
and all my petals trembled.

When you went down
into the earth when you
died into the earth when they
cut you into pieces
and floated you on the Nile
when they pierced you
and the sea flowed from your side
I searched for you forever
I re-membered you I
washed you and wrapped you
with the spices the sweet
the bitter, and I

wailed, I raised
the spring floods I
made the earth quake I
split the sky I
tore the temple veil
and my garments and my
hair my face my thighs
and the people wept

with me and I
brought you back from the dead
through my gates into my arms I
brought you back
you rose for me.

Now the pews creak
The priest reads the story slowly.
The green corn is forgotten
and the brown dirt. The story says
the Roman powers who once lined
the road from Rome to Ostia
with corpses on crosses whine
Aw come on, we don't wanna kill him
Oh well all right if you people insist.

No, you say, standing behind me,
It wasn't like that. My people
didn't kill me, and they forgot
the part about you. You
tell the story now.
You.

And the palms of my hands
begin to throb and sing
and I say silently
I will.

In the Temple of the Child

In the temple of the child
there are doves and snakes
and a baby tiger.
The snakes drink milk from a small table
made just for them
like in the palaces on Crete.

The temple of the child is an inside place
full of light. Light like when your mother
shone her belly at the naked sun
before you were born. Gold and rose
and a watery dream of sky
so the blue in the temple
always carries a hint of gold and green.
The earth floor is red,
all the blood of birth and moon is mixed
and ground fine as powder.
When you add water, you get clay
for the child to play with. She makes
small worlds around her feet.

In the temple of the child
my mother relaxes on the throne of Isis
which is sometimes a comfortable couch.
The shining horns sit lightly in her hair
and she wears the blue mantle of Mary
— that blue I told you about —
over a gold robe, warm and soft
as sand in the sun.

When my mother looks at the child
she smiles, the way she smiled at me
the last time I saw her just before

she died, the way she smiled at me
when they put me into her arms
for the first time.

She has her own thoughts
as she watches the doves, as she walks
on the shore of the sea inside the temple.
But when the child turns to her
her lap is an altar.
Her arms hold the child's head
next to the seashell sound of her heart.

For formal portraits the child sits
on the mother's lap, their faces close together,
one arm each around the other,
the other open wide to the world.
The colors swim around them —
terra cotta, green, gold, blue,
light dappled by the doves' wings.
The tiger curls at their feet.
The snakes lap their milk.

Over the altar there are words.
The letters are alive,
running, flying, moving shapes,
a hieroglyphic ticker tape.
The words say:
This is my beloved daughter
in whom I am well-pleased.

The Gift of the Garden

There is a gift in the garden
not the pretty daytime place,
but that other where you said,
Watch with me and everyone
fell asleep and god was silent
as the birds with their heads
under their wings
and you were alone
with your terrible knowing.

After we drain the cup
that will not pass
some of us are still alive
but not the same
not ever again.
We have the gift of the garden.
And when someone says
Watch with me, we know
we will stay awake.

The United Voices Gospel Choir

When the choir sang
Jesus burst into the room
through our hearts
like they were the swinging doors
of the soul's saloon.
He walked on water again
as we shifted his sweet weight
from side to side.
He brought together
right and left, black and white
with each clap of our hands.
And the sweat on each shining face
were the tears he wept
turned into a glad shout.

Dream

FOR JO RENBECK

On a low table
sit the horns of Isis
the horns are the crescent moon
come to earth
come to the coffee klatch
of the women of the world
but instead of cups and clutter
there are the horns
white as moon
white as bone
stark beneath garlands of flowers
with big bodacious blooms.
A voice says,
the flowers are the Mother
they are us, blossoming
beneath the blossoms
the maiden the moon
the old one
bone.

≈73

The Temple of Isis

When I sit on the banks of the Hudson
I know I am in your temple
you who rose with the dog star over the Nile
who gave birth among the reeds
under the shelter of Uazit's cobra hood.
You glide in your moon-shaped boat
and Nile becomes Tiber Thames
Mohawk Mississippi till your river
finds me here at sunset in November
watching waves laced with fire
counting the four black guardian rocks
that rise from the river
under a breast of Catskill, Egyptian blue.
I watch the tide thrust one way
and the current pull another
and the water swirl around
and around and I say, Isis
Almighty Isis, welcome home.

November Trees

In November when I see them
gathered grey, brown remnants
of leaf curling and wisping at their tips,
pooled in laps of root, the trees
look like their own ghosts
like lingering smoke, like incense
thick and sinuous. With the
green veil stripped away, I see
the whole trunk sways, as if
the trees are davening, these trees
who teach what temple columns are.

7

HEART WILD AND GREEN

Sower

I keep scattering seeds
some demented sower
who hasn't quite figured out
how agriculture works, hell,
it wasn't so long ago
I was wandering with my herds
or just chasing whatever was around
lemmings, woolly mammoths and what not
picking a few berries
along the way.

Now here I am
with my sower's sack
full of words, these gifts
from god I somehow harvested.
I want to share the wealth.
I want to feed the world, but
where the hell is that fertile crescent
or even — goddamn — a crack
in the cement?

Wind take these words.
Birds eat them
and crap them out
on some ground where
they can grow.

Widow's Mite

Untempted by genuine diamonds
or trashy trinkets I turn to the antiquities.
I choose a widow's mite.
Jesus said: She gave all she had.
That's all I want to do.

Pilgrim Feet

All night my first night back from pilgrimage
I dream of feet. Feet on the Temple Mount,
flocks of shoes surrounding
our guide whose earliest memory
from just after the Six Days War
is playing with shoes while her parents
went to the rock where the Ark of the Covenant
might have stood, where Abraham
would have sacrificed his son
if the angel hadn't touched down
on the rock where later Mohammed
blasted off for seventh heaven
leaving his foot-print behind
for barefoot pilgrims to touch,
their tired feet caressed by thick,
new carpet given by some potentate
to match the King of Jordan's golden dome,
carpets like the ones in my childhood shrine
the house of childless neighbors who let us
tread luxuriant meadows of oriental pile
if we left our shoes at the door.
My feet remember that cloudy softness
till they are crammed swollen and blistered
back into shoes to walk on stones
stones on stones on stones
where Jesus walked, his feet dusty and sore,
crying out for a woman's tears
and hair, her costly oils.
He knew what mattered after that
and taught his disciples to kneel down
and love each other's feet.

Walking on Water

When Jesus walked on the water
maybe he waded out on some huge
tidal flat, just a shiny inch of water
giving back the sky
cloud for cloud, blue for blue
now and then a shoal of sand
pink at sunset when the sun
squeezes out its last sweet juice.
Then the water turns dusky,
hidden things come out
and scuttle around his toes.

Maybe he didn't,
but when I walk out with the tide,
the sea calling to me, walk
walk on the water walk
walk on forever
it's no less a miracle.

Love Song to My Body

FOR KAREN HOLTSLAG

Body when we dance we are hearing
the earth we are seeing its songs
we are its waves and its whirlings
and its rock bottom
when we sing we are huge inside
we are the first cave
we are the lighting of the stars
we are the sound of the river
flowing in the dark.

Sun

The sun loves me.
Oh yeah, I know, like the Bible says
the sun shines on good and evil alike
and I like that about old Sol.
But when the sun shines on me
touching my cheek like a lover
turning my heart wild and green
lighting my crown like the 4th of July
grand finale, I know
the sun loves me
and on behalf of the planet
I take it very personally.

Hands

My hands meet at my heart.
The tiny chasm between my palms
contains a fire, holds all the sounds
I hear, the gunshot
and the deer's last leap.
My hands at my heart
the cavern of my palms
make an opening for my lover
the one who leaps in me
who holds me cupped in flame
where I float an embryo
a seed bursting in bright
dark ecstasy.

Trust

I put my trust in mystery

I am a bird on the breast of the wind
in my throat the wind is a song
I put my trust in the wind.

I am a seed in his hand
I am held in her womb
the earth feeds me
and I am her food.
I put my trust in the earth.

Under the wave
in the deep places I shine.
I have seen the moon
from the bottom of the sea
I put my trust in the water.

My palms burn where his were pierced.
I am the bread she bakes
I put my trust in the fire.

He puts his hand between my breasts
I am his.
She takes me on her lap
she shows me where the world begins.
I am hers.

When my heart is undefended
I am safe
living or dying
I am safe.

I put my trust where it belongs.

8

STONES THAT RING THE FIRE

Broken Home

Everything is here to stay,
one with the place we forgot to call home.
Shake the dust from your feet
and it remains the ground beneath them.
There is only change, river becoming rain
becoming river, fallen leaves
feeding the roots of trees feeding leaves,
the slow redemption of rot.
It is the indestructible that destroys,
the things that won't break down
that may break us — unless
we break first, as an egg shatters
to release the bird
or a seed splits open and
takes hold in the earth.

Healing Song

At your feet, the earth
In your womb, the sea
In your belly, the fire
At your center, the sun
In your heart, the flower
In your throat, the sky
On your brow, the moon
At your crown, the star
In your hands, the earth.

Omens

FOR TOM COWAN

Who am I, North?
>You are the wind
>>a black man waiting
>>>for a ride.

Where do I come from, East?
>You come from the light
>>from the river's
>>>rising tide.

What is my power, South?
>To be the stones that ring the fire
>>to know that something
>>>must yield.

Where am I going, West?
>To the dark tree with two strong trunks
>>to the sapling springing
>>>from the rock.

Our Other Selves

We breathe together
in and out, in and out,
tossing tides of air
back and forth between us
in a rhythm so perfect
we forget it's there,
but that's not all.

The trees root for us.
They know the unfiltered
taste of rain and dirt
the taste of light.
The weather comes and goes
hugely in their heights.
Their depths hold the soil
of continents.

What can we do for the trees
our other selves?
We can dance, lift our footloose
soles and tap out a rhythm
on our common ground.
We can listen with all our heart
to the song of the wind in the leaves
and sing it back.

Miracle

I expect a miracle
when I ride the train
and see the lush, chaotic
landscape flying by,
hectic with trash and bloom,
always growing back,
defying gravity
with its green obsession.
I expect a miracle
at every moment
of my own.

Perseid Showers

Today I see a stone in the driveway
where the wheels roll
over and over
grinding it into the dirt.
The light hits just right,
a million flecks of mica shine
as if all the stars of August
have fallen here.

The End of the Worlds

Just before the fog lifts from the river
a duck walks on water and disappears
the way ducks do in Chinese scrolls
I walk to the very edge of the river
I see white water moving
I see white cloud moving
there is a place that doesn't move
there is a place where water and sky collide
I see my blindness
I see a hair-crack in my cornea
I see the end of the worlds.

Healing Over

FOR DONNA

See how the earth heals over
new leaves, lush tangled understory
poison ivy protecting the scarred places.
See how the earth comes back
each spring
drinking rain and light
giving them form.
See how the earth wants to live
how soft and insistent it is.

You are earth
a catastrophic seed bed
like the redwoods after a forest fire
or the ashen mulch
of volcanic eruption.
Let yourself heal over,
let yourself grow back.
Someday birds will sing
in you.